HUMBUG AND HAPPINESS

HUMBUG AND HAPPINESS

An advent study with the classic movie
A Christmas Carol (Scrooge)

SHEILA JACOBS

DARTON·LONGMAN+TODD

First published in Great Britain in 2019 by
Darton, Longman and Todd Ltd
1 Spencer Court
140–142 Wandsworth High Street
London SW18 4JJ

ISBN 978-0-232-53410-8

All Bible quotes taken from the NIV 2011 UK unless
otherwise indicated.

A catalogue record for this book is available from the
British Library.

Timings given for film clips are approximate

Designed and produced by Judy Linard

Printed and bound in Great Britain by Bell & Bain Ltd, Glasgow

CONTENTS

INTRODUCTION

The shops are full of tinsel, Santas, gingerbread lattes, fake fir trees and every kind of new toy. Christmas cards are on sale, promising pretty winterlands with quaint, snow-covered cottages nestling around picturesque churches, and robins perched on frosty branches. Ah, it must be … September!

Oops! Does that sound cynical?

I'm not sure when 'humbug' crept into my Christmas experience, but it did. When I was a child, Christmas was a special time. I loved travelling to visit my grandparents, who lived some distance from us. They always had an impressive display of cards strung on ribbons decorating the living room, a large, real tree in the corner and underneath, the most interesting bit: presents, and some of them with my name on the tag. So Christmas was a time of grandparents, extended family, playing with my cousins, watching TV together and having a lovely dinner.

The run-up to the day itself was never uneventful. I was usually chosen to be the narrator in school nativity plays. I remember kids dressed as angels with cardboard and tinsel halos, and the happiness of glitter and glue and cotton wool as we attempted to make our own Christmas cards. Oh, and then there was the carol service.

I think I started to feel a creeping sense of 'humbug' when, over a period of several years, three people I cared about passed away around Christmastime. Or maybe I just got jaded!

Did you notice that Jesus didn't really enter my childhood Christmas thinking? I probably thought about the baby in the manger during the carols and nativity play, but 'Advent' was just a word for a certain type of calendar. I only remember going to church twice when I was around ten, then being obliged to go with the school when I was older, and three forays into church-land when I was a teen. My Sunday school was, in effect, my granny, who told me stories about Jesus when I stayed with her during the summer holidays. I believed in him from an early age and would even have considered myself 'a Christian', having had an encounter with him when I was around fourteen, but I didn't understand what it truly meant to follow him – although by my late teens I had an idea that I wasn't living as I should.

So, Christmas for me wasn't about Jesus. Strangely, I became even more entrenched in humbug when I surrendered my life to him at the age of twenty-five and finally understood that he really was the 'reason for the season'. At that point it seemed to me that Christmas was more of a pagan festival than anything to do with the coming of the Son of God, as man – God's amazing rescue mission. The commercialisation of the season was so evident to my newly opened eyes: the manipulative advertising, the clamouring for more 'stuff' to ensure our 'perfect' day, the frantic last-minute shopping, the angst over the right-size turkey, the fluffiest potatoes! Then the inevitable comedown for so many, when the bills arrived …

I'm beginning to sound like Scrooge! What a character – one of the greatest in all fiction, in my opinion; full of humbug until some supernatural encounters change his way of thinking, not only impacting his own life, but changing that of others, and bringing great happiness to all.

The Christmas season may be one you enjoy. Perhaps for you, the happiness far outweighs the humbug; you're not Scrooge-like in any way! Or maybe, like many others, you find Christmas difficult; perhaps the hardest time of the year. My own approach to Christmas is slowly changing. These days I try not to let cynicism ruin the celebration – although I still don't like the commercialisation – but neither do I focus on the comforting familiarity of nativities and carols, a half-remembered romanticism left over from childhood. For me, Christmas isn't even about the excitement of presents (well … I do like presents), it's about Jesus – seeking his presence among the celebrations. Because as I continue my walk with him, I realise that I have to constantly look for him among all the 'stuff' of life that threatens to crowd him out; especially, perhaps, during the craziness of December, when I really do need to rediscover, amid the stress and the hurry and the twinkling fairy lights, the true Light of the world, and remember how thankful I am for his first coming, as I await his second Advent.

It's easy to get distracted, especially at this time of the year, so it's good to be able to set aside time to be with Jesus, to refocus. What better way than to enjoy a great Christmas movie, and to use this to encourage us to consider what Advent is really all about.

There have been many adaptations of Charles Dickens' famous novel of 1843, but the one we are looking at here, with the delightful Alastair Sim as Ebenezer Scrooge, is a classic. If you are familiar with Dickens' work, this may inspire you to read the original story again (or for the first time, if Dickens hasn't been 'your thing'). The 1951 film version of the famous tale is so well known, you have probably seen it before – maybe countless times. But as you watch it again, look out for what God may be saying to you through this Christmas treat.

Released as *A Christmas Carol* in the United States, it introduces us to the miserly misery and his world. Dickens, of course, wrote his books in such a way as to highlight the social issues of his day, and this film speaks great truth to us even now. The importance of generosity of spirit rather than selfish living; forgiveness; restoration – there are so many themes here, many of which I hope we can address.

As well as Sim, glance at the cast list and see how many popular British actors you recognise from yesteryear: Michael Hordern, George Cole, Patrick Macnee, Hermione Baddeley, Jack Warner, Hattie Jacques. And, of course, we are introduced to some great fictional creations, including the Cratchit family, with Scrooge's long-suffering clerk, Bob Cratchit (Mervyn Johns), and Cratchit's lame, sick son, the unforgettable Tiny Tim, played here by Glyn Dearman.

The way the film is constructed is interesting. There's quite a spooky start, ominous in its bleakness, leading into the supernatural encounters. Scrooge is almost a caricature; we can be in no doubt of his hard-hearted personality; he has no compassion for the poor. But it's only as the curtain is drawn back and we find out what made him this way that we begin to truly understand him. He becomes more 'real' and eventually, quite lovable. Alistair Sim plays the part with suitable tragedy and comedy. In this story, we see plainly that selfishness, idolising wealth and withdrawing into his own very small world has led to alienation, and a deathly loneliness. There is no lasting contentment and fulfilment to be found in Scrooge's cold existence. The film suggests that generosity, love and forgiveness are the traits we should nurture. Indeed, they are what make us human.

This is a story about 'ghosts' – the spirit of Jacob Marley visits his old business partner. He is a spirit in torment, due to the poor way he has lived, condemned to wander the earth. He has come to warn Scrooge that he needs to repent to avoid the same fate, and tells him that three other spirits will visit him. These are the Spirit of Christmas Past, the Spirit of Christmas Present and the Spirit of Christmas Yet to Come. The spirits duly arrive, and the past, present and future are laid out before the rather bewildered and ultimately penitent Ebenezer.

Obviously, there are huge theological

differences between what is shown in the film and what the Bible teaches. Spiritualism – the occult, séances, mediumship – was very popular in Dickens' Victorian Britain. But spiritualism – attempting to contact the dead – has been practised for far longer than that. As far back as the Old Testament, Saul, Israel's first king, sought out a medium and apparently encountered the spirit of Samuel the prophet as a result (1 Samuel 28). Saul had actually banished mediums from the land, obeying the Lord's commands in Leviticus 19:31, Leviticus 20:6, 27 and Deuteronomy 18:10-12. Whether or not Saul really met a 'ghost', we cannot tell, but it is plain from Scripture that God, who loves us, does not want his people to try to contact the dead; this is not his will for us. There can be no doubt that there is a spiritual, unseen world; the Bible speaks of angels who worship and serve God – but it also speaks of an enemy: demons, a satanic kingdom that opposes God and his people. Opening a door to the enemy in disobedience to God's will is therefore not a good idea.

It seems that Saul's attempt to contact Samuel was an act born out of desperation. But the Word of God advocates that rather than trying to contact the dead or any other spiritual 'being' when we need assurance, comfort or guidance, we should go to God himself, through Jesus Christ. Under the old covenant, this was impossible, except for a chosen few; a study of the role of the high priest and the tabernacle and Temple in the Old Testament and the entrance into God's holy presence is well worth it, if you have the time (after Christmas!), because it shows us just how much Jesus accomplished for us on the cross. He came to set us free from the old ways of sacrifice for sins that separate us from our holy God, becoming sin for us (2 Corinthians 5:21). The Temple curtain, dividing the holiest place from the rest, was torn in two when Jesus died, signifying that we have access through his blood into God's presence (Matthew 27:51).

So, for the purposes of our Advent study, we must see past (or through!) the 'ghosts' to a greater truth. We observe that Jacob Marley is reaping what he sowed while he was alive (Galatians 6:7-10). The principle is quite clear: repent – turn from this old way of living. Live new. But of course, we do that as we come to Jesus, have our uncleanness washed away, and enter into the life-giving presence of a Father who loves us. We don't earn salvation by 'being good'; as Ephesians 2:8-9 tells us: 'For it is by grace [God's free, unearned favour] you have been saved, through faith – and this is not from yourselves, it is the gift of God – not by works, so that no one can boast.' Good deeds may (and should) flow from a heart changed by God, the fruit of a whole new life, but it's only by accepting Christ's sacrifice that we can be made right with God.

This book has been written for personal use, but you may wish to look at it with a group – there are suggestions for how to do this at the back. It isn't a 'course', and you don't have to read the chapters as four Advent 'weeks'. Read it in the way that suits you best during this busy period. There are places to pause for thought, to think about themes, and Advent connections. I have suggested clips to illustrate points; you don't have to watch them, but you may find it beneficial to play a clip and read the 'think about' comment. (Please note that all timings given are approximate.) At the end of the chapters you will find ideas for activities, reflection and prayer. It might be a good idea to use the book as part of your quiet time, if you have one. Before you start, I suggest you watch the film all the way through. It's available on DVD – I expect you know someone who has a copy! Grab some of your favourite snacks, and enjoy.

This tale of humbug and happiness is about reviewing the past, and will help us to think about how our present choices are impacting the future. Jesus came – a long-anticipated Messiah, rejected by many – is here in our present, and will come again. My prayer for you as you watch this wonderful movie and read this book is that you, like me, will let this thought-provoking story challenge your attitudes and actions; and that this Advent season, you will have a life-changing encounter with the living God.

Sheila Jacobs
Halstead, Essex

CHAPTER ONE
THE CHAINS OF LIFE

PREPARE YOURSELF

Do you enjoy Christmas? What do you like about it, especially? If not, what do you dislike, and why?

TO START

'He doesn't trust anyone!' 'She's so reserved!' 'What on earth did I say that made him react like that?'

It's easy to judge people, especially if we don't really know them! But if we knew their backstory, we might find it explained a great deal about their sometimes puzzling behaviour – and our own! For example, imagine someone has had a teacher/parent/carer who seemed to blame them for everything. Years later, perceived criticism from anyone else may incite an over-the-top response. In effect, that person is responding to today's situations based on something they have experienced in the past.

That person you find difficult to get on with (or maybe *you* are the difficult one!) – did they (or we) start out that way? What changed them (or us)?

As we begin to get to know Ebenezer Scrooge, we will soon find out that there's a backstory to his miserliness and locked-in coldness. Everyone has a backstory … sometimes it's worth remembering that before we jump to conclusions.

PAUSE FOR THOUGHT

Do you know anyone who seems a bit 'prickly' in their attitude? Why not pray for them?

WATCH: 1:58–3:22

As we begin the adventure into Ebenezer Scrooge's journey of self-revelation, we can see right from the start that he is a miserable man with apparently no conscience.

Scrooge manifestly sees Christmas as a total inconvenience. It stops him from doing his business. It's all humbug. A man owes him £20 and begs for more time to pay, but Scrooge treats him with unfeeling cruelty.

If you watched the film's intro before the clip,

you might have had a feeling of menace from quite an ominous version of *Hark! the Herald Angels Sing.*

THINK ABOUT

Does this remind you of the parable Jesus told in Luke 12:13-21 about the rich fool? He gathered together all his wealth, but his life would soon be over. Then who would benefit from his hoarded goods? Jesus has already warned his listeners about being on their guard against greed, for 'life does not consist in an abundance of possessions'. That, as we will see, is actually the story of Scrooge.

It's great to have a home, a car, material possessions, and it's wonderful to be able to help others out of our blessings, but how easy it is to begin to put 'stuff' in the place of God in our hearts. It's possible to start off with good intentions, determined to keep a balance, but if we're not careful, life can all too soon become all about *money. Things. Possessions.*

I don't watch a lot of TV, but when I do, I tend to 'mute' the adverts. Do we believe possessing that new car/furniture is totally necessary to our well-being? Have we bought into a materialistic lie that we can't be happy without the latest … (fill in the blank)?

PAUSE FOR THOUGHT
Reality check! How far do you believe that owning 'things' makes you happy?

WATCH: 3:40–5:34

In this clip we see two men visiting with Scrooge. His partner, Jacob Marley, has been dead for seven years. They have apparently come for a donation from Scrooge towards the poor and destitute at Christmas. These kind-hearted altruists see a bigger picture than Ebenezer does. His rebuke, 'Are there no prisons? … And the union workhouses, are they still in operation?' is chilling.

The men want to offer help to the poor during the richness of the season. Scrooge's reply is that he supports establishments that he has mentioned – and he refuses to help. When his visitors suggest that some would rather die than go to these establishments, he remarks that they should do so and 'decrease the surplus population'. His words will come back to haunt him, quite literally. He is constantly occupied with his own world. He does not look outwards with any pity.

This is such an interesting piece – and sets the scene for what will happen later. We are, right at the outset, in no doubt of Scrooge's nature.

THINK ABOUT

This period in Britain's history was a time of great turbulence. I remember studying Economic History at school and learning how the Industrial Revolution of the late-eighteenth and early-nineteenth centuries meant that life was radically changing as people shifted from the countryside into the towns, and industry began to change the face of the nation.

I recall talking with an elderly friend years ago about workhouses – still remembered and greatly feared. My granny, born in 1906, the daughter of Victorian parents, often told me of her Christmas presents – fruit, nuts and one year a doll with a wax face ... which melted by the fire. Today, I wonder what we imagine when we think of 'poverty'. Someone in the Third World, who cannot get access to clean water? People sleeping on the streets in cold weather? Or do we think someone is 'poor' because they don't have a smartphone?

It's true, too, that Christmas is a time when those who are in any kind of 'want' may feel it most. Not just financially, but in other ways too. For instance, those who have no family, or have suffered loss – the empty place at the table. At a time when the media in particular seems to enforce the picture of the ideal Christmas, complete with family, friends, soft glowing lights and tables overflowing with good things, those without resources or loved ones can certainly feel the full force of any lack. Christmas seems to exacerbate the emptiness.

PAUSE FOR THOUGHT
Is there anyone you know who you consider 'poor' in some way? How can you help them/pray for them this Christmas?

WATCH: 5:37-6:37

Now we are introduced to the delightful Fred, Ebenezer's nephew. He is full of joy and wishes his uncle merry Christmas. Scrooge remarks that keeping Christmas has never done his nephew any good – by now, we are understanding that his benchmark for 'good' is 'wealthy'. Fred has apparently married against his uncle's wishes, for love, and his wife is poor. Fred is happy, though! Despite his uncle's churlishness he responds with kindness. He invites Scrooge to Christmas dinner. But it's all humbug to Scrooge!

THINK ABOUT

I like how Scrooge's nephew refuses to let his uncle dampen his spirits. He still holds out an olive branch, even though he is being rejected. I wonder how many of us would have walked away from such an unpleasant man.

When we are hurt we can easily respond 'in kind': you rejected me, I will reject you. Of course, Jesus doesn't act in that way. He was abandoned by his disciples when he was arrested, but after the crucifixion and resurrection, what happened? Did he appear merely to tell them he wanted nothing more to do with them? No. In John 21 we don't see him pointing the finger at his disciples, we see him cooking them breakfast! And he gently reinstates the one who denied him three times.

It could be that there are times you would like to walk away from God – and from other people. Jesus knows what it's like to be rejected but he doesn't give up on us. He says he will never leave or forsake us (Isaiah 53:3; Hebrews 13:5).

We will look further at this whole theme of rejection in the next chapter.

PAUSE FOR THOUGHT
Have you walked away from God?
Or from someone else? Why?

WATCH: 7:05-10:20; 10:29-50
Here we are introduced to Tim, the lame little son of Bob Cratchit, Scrooge's clerk. Tim is

looking through a toy shop window with some delight. There's a moment of poignancy when someone buys a boat, and Tim looks longingly on – his family clearly can't afford to buy him these toys. But Tim's cheery demeanour quickly returns. This scene is a good contrast for what follows: Scrooge's attitude to having to give Cratchit Christmas Day off – and still having to pay him a day's wages! But for all his poverty and his employer's harsh treatment, Bob Cratchit is as sunny-natured as his son.

As for Scrooge, he isn't even kind to himself: in the second clip, in the inn, we see he wants more bread, but when he finds out it costs a little extra, won't buy it.

THINK ABOUT

I shared earlier about my 'jaded' feelings around Christmas. But what about you? Do you feel a spark of excitement about the season – and about life? Or has disappointment, disillusionment, robbed you of your joy … or even your faith? Remember back to the dreams of childhood. Which of those dreams have been fulfilled? Which might yet be? What are your hopes for the coming year? Did God give you his vision for your life, at the start of your Christian walk? Do you need to ask him about this now?

When Jesus spoke about the kingdom of God,

he said we should have a child-like (not child*ish*) attitude – one of trust (Matthew 18:1-3). Perhaps your trust in God has been damaged in some way. Is it time to ask him to renew in you a child-like faith in a heavenly Father who loves you?

PAUSE FOR THOUGHT
In what way can you be especially kind to yourself this Christmastime?

WATCH: 11:03-20:37

Scrooge begins to encounter the supernatural at this point. Going home, his door knocker takes the appearance of Jacob Marley's face. Scrooge is still in 'humbug' mode even when his name is eerily spoken and it becomes apparent that there are ghostly goings-on! Ever the cynic … sitting alone, eating gruel …

Then the door flies open, and here is the first supernatural visit.

Jacob Marley, Scrooge's deceased business partner, is wearing a great chain. Jacob points out that Scrooge doesn't believe in him. Scrooge gives an answer that always makes me smile: that what he is experiencing is probably down to indigestion!

Scared into believing what he's encountering,

'worldly' Scrooge listens to his partner and asks him why he's there.

Jacob talks about the chain, which he made himself while he was alive, and how Scrooge is forging a much bigger one! He tells Scrooge about how he is condemned to walk the earth after death. What he is saying is that because he didn't share in the lives of others when he lived, he is condemned to watch from afar now he is dead, regretting, in torment, with no peace or rest that he can never be part of the happiness he might have had if he had lived differently – for others; and it's too late to change anything.

Of course, Jacob has come to warn Scrooge that he has a chance to escape Marley's fate. Three spirits will visit him …

THINK ABOUT

The idea of forging a chain we carry into death is quite sobering. Hebrews 9:27 tells us: 'people are destined to die once, and after that to face judgment' which doesn't appear to teach that unrepentant spirits roam the earth in torment (and also gives no leeway to any thought of reincarnation). There is going to be a day of reckoning. Jesus took the penalty for our wrongdoing – the chains we have made for ourselves, if you like – on himself on the cross. Jesus said, famously, in John 3:16-17: 'For God so loved the world that he gave his one and only Son, that whoever believes in him shall not perish but have eternal life. For God did not send his Son into the world to condemn the world, but to save the world through him.' Unlike Marley, we needn't have to pay the price for our own sin. Jesus has done that for us. Thank God!

There is no condemnation when we come to Christ (Romans 8:1). Our sins are judged and condemned *in Jesus*. He promises in John 6:37 that he will never turn away anybody who comes to him. We might regret many aspects of our past, but we can surrender this to Jesus, knowing he will forgive, accept and restore us. We don't need to be bound like Jacob Marley, because Jesus sets us free (John 8:36; Galatians 5:1). We may feel as if we are bound by chains that someone else has placed around us. If that's the case, it could be time to examine the nature of these chains and, with God, explore the whole area of what it truly means to live in the freedom offered by Jesus.

I don't believe God scares us into believing in him, as Marley's ghost does with Scrooge; rather, he *invites* us into relationship. In the story of the woman at the well in John's Gospel, Jesus knew everything about her dysfunctional background, but far from condemning her, he came alongside and offered her something better; eternal life, the 'living water' of the Spirit of God (John 4:10,13-14).

Jacob Marley is not in hell, but he seems to represent a separation from God in regret and torment that seems pretty hellish to me. This scene really is thought-provoking – but not without hope. At least, not for Scrooge.

It may also motivate us to tell others about Jesus. Eternal separation from God, or the new life and relationship with the Lord that is ours when we come to him? The invitation is there. Let's make sure others know about it.

PAUSE FOR THOUGHT
Imagine Jesus, on the cross, wrapped around with chains we have forged on earth. Because he wore them, we don't have to. Stay as long as you can in that place of surrender and gratitude.

ADVENT CONNECTION

Read: Luke 1:26-38
> … The angel went to [Mary] and said, 'Greetings, you who are highly favoured! The Lord is with you.'
> Mary was greatly troubled at his words … But

the angel said to her, 'Do not be afraid, Mary, you have found favour with God. You will conceive and give birth to a son, and you are to call him Jesus. He will be great and will be called the Son of the Most High. The Lord God will give him the throne of his father David, and he will reign over Jacob's descendants for ever; his kingdom will never end ...'

Mary wasn't visited by a ghost. Neither was her supernatural visitor someone who made her fearful – rather, he urged her not to be afraid. Still, as with Scrooge's encounter, the point of the conversation was salvation. In verse 46 of Luke 1, Mary rejoices in God, her 'Saviour' – but this wasn't just about her own life; it was about the world. Luke 53:6 tells us 'We all, like sheep, have gone astray' but that God has laid our iniquity, that which would separate us from him, on the One who would come to save us. Yes, God had a plan. He sent an angel to talk to Mary and invite her to be a big part of it.

Imagine what it must have been like for a teenage girl, betrothed to Joseph, to have a supernatural interruption into her presumably quiet world. True, supernatural events had already happened in her family. Her relative, Elizabeth, was miraculously pregnant; her son, John, would have his own part to play in the events to come, as the prophesied herald of the coming Messiah.

And now, Mary was going to have a baby. He would be God's own Son, conceived by the Holy Spirit. In light of the fact that she would face huge consequences in her time and culture for becoming pregnant outside of marriage, her answer is astonishing: 'I am the Lord's servant … May your word to me be fulfilled.' Total surrender to God – trusting him to make everything work out.

I feel God often challenges me through 'pictures'. I like looking at water from the shore, but I am no sailor! Yet, this was an idea that slipped into my mind recently. If I was offered a place in a small boat that looked pretty leaky and unsafe, but Jesus was in that boat, would I choose to step aboard? Or stay on the apparent safety of the shore?

Mary really did step out. She took a huge risk. But then, a perplexed Joseph, after some initial and understandable doubt, was encouraged in the truth by more supernatural intervention (Matthew 1:18-24).

Does God intervene in our lives today? Does he still heal, set free and deliver people from the oppression of darkness? I believe he does; he doesn't change. We may see the kingdom of God breaking into lives in all sorts of ways.

But the biggest miracle of all is that the Divine humbled himself and became a child, sharing in our humanity (Philippians 2:6-8) – but not our sin, overcoming temptation, so he can be compassionate in our failures. We can always approach him when we need help (Hebrews 4:15-16; Hebrews 7:25).

God broke into our chaotic lives in the first coming of Jesus. He had decided to save us before we even knew we needed a Saviour. Indeed, we were his enemies, and are reconciled to God only by the death of Jesus (Romans 5:10). That God effected a rescue at such enormous cost to himself is staggering, isn't it? He didn't just write us off. How precious we must be to him, all unique, individual, made in his image (Genesis 1:27). Jesus came to offer us a way back into friendship with God – friendship humanity lost when we turned away from him in the Garden of Eden, disobeying his kind command, hiding ourselves from him, covering our shame (Genesis 3). We still have the propensity to hide from God, running from him rather than to him when we get it wrong, trying to hide our shame, as if he doesn't know all about it! Yet the safest place is in his presence. There we will find love and acceptance and forgiveness.

In the presence of God, can we keep on in

ways that offend him and hurt others? No. As we come to Jesus for the help we need, asking for the strength to live for him in the power of his Holy Spirit, and experiencing his presence, we will soon find out that 'sin' gets in the way of relationship. We will discover the increasing need to drop the 'stuff' that alienates us from the presence of God, so we can become ever-closer to him. If we choose to keep running, we are, in essence, rejecting the everlasting One who calls us to 'come', the eternal Life, Jesus; and to reject him is to reject love itself.

PAUSE FOR THOUGHT

- 'Do not be afraid … you have found favour with God … May your word to me be fulfilled.' Do any of these phrases speak especially to you?
- Given the choice, would you step aboard a 'leaky' boat with Jesus? Or remain on the 'safety' of the shore?
- In times of stress or anxiety or when you 'get it wrong', do you run from Jesus, or run to him? Do you need to run to him now?

ACTIVITY SUGGESTIONS

- Do you feel 'chained' by anything? Can you talk to Jesus about whatever you feel binds you, and ask him to set you free? If possible, share with a trusted Christian friend or leader.
- Write a letter to God, talking about everything and anything. Believe he 'reads' it. He knows you and he loves you, and he is concerned about every part of your life. He invites you to follow him – one step at a time.

REFLECTION

What might God be saying to you so far in Scrooge's story? Think about keeping a journal and jotting down anything you believe God might say to you while you read this book. One thing you could be thinking about already is how much Jesus loves you. We may alienate ourselves from his presence, but he is always waiting for us to come to him so he might restore us to himself. It's worth reflecting on Ephesians 2:6-7, which tells us we are seated in the heavenly places with Jesus. How does that scripture challenge you in regard to how you view yourself, your life, how much God loves you, today?

PRAYER

*Lord, I thank and praise you that you came to earth
that very first Christmas in order to set us free. My
sins were condemned in you, and I need no longer be
bound by them or separated from you. Jesus, you did
everything the Father asked of you so I could be your
friend and know you now and forever. Thank you
for forgiving me, Lord! Amen.*

CHAPTER TWO
IN THE PAST

PREPARE YOURSELF

Have you ever gone back to a place you used to know well (a school, somewhere you lived, a favourite holiday resort), and found it vastly changed? How did you feel about that – or about the changing nature of your own area, such as new buildings/roads?

TO START

Scrooge's first encounter with a spirit (other than Jacob Marley's) is with the Spirit of Christmas Past … specifically of *Scrooge's* past.

Here we learn all about Scrooge's history – just why he is such a humbug of a man. It's a tragic tale. It seems Scrooge was a lonely child not wanted at home by his father. We see Scrooge as a forgotten boy, all alone … till his sister arrives.

When I was a child, my family moved around the UK, and I finished up going to eight different schools. As the 'new kid', it often took me a while to fit in, and there were, inevitably, rejections.

I don't know what your childhood was like. Maybe you had a good relationship with your parents – maybe you didn't. It could be that one (or both) was not consistently in your life. Perhaps you can even relate to Scrooge's experience of a distant, absent, rejecting parent. I think it's true that the experience we have of our earthly father in particular can affect our view of our heavenly Father. For example, if you found you couldn't rely on a parent, you may now find it difficult to rely on God.

If our experience has been negative, as Scrooge's was, we need to remember that while people are fallible and may let us down (and we let them down too), Jesus is totally reliable.

Sadly, these days, when families are so often fragmented, the sense of rejection, real or imagined, can have knock-on effects into someone's later life. It can make us build up a wall around ourselves – a barrier called 'self-protection'. That's what we really see Scrooge doing in his young life; although subsequent choices make his path to loneliness rather more inevitable than it might have been. We have already seen that while Scrooge rejects his sister's son, Fred doesn't reject him, which is incredibly generous of him.

In Scrooge's backstory we can see that he loved his sister. She was his champion, on his side. Who do you champion? And who champions you?

I wonder what part of your own past you would like to revisit, given the chance. Or do you revisit it anyway, in your mind? Even without Scrooge's supernatural companion to accompany us, we may spend a lot of time dwelling in the past. It can become a place of comfort if we are going through a time of uncertainty or loss. While it's great to have good memories, when we spend too much of our time looking back, our vision can become distorted. We can be tempted to view bygone days through rose-tinted lenses, and find ourselves retreating ever more to this 'safe' but sometimes rather skewed version of the world. If you find yourself lingering too long in memories, perhaps re-evaluate – why are you there?

Conversely, we can become stuck in the bad stuff: hurts, rejection and damage from years past. But if we allow the past to continually define us, letting it shape our current decisions, our thought-life and how we think about ourselves, we are giving the event or people that damaged us power over our precious 'now'. If we think of our lives as gardens, with God planting beautiful things in them (as well as pruning; John 15:1-3), it's like letting someone or something from long ago walk all over our precious garden, perhaps pouring weed killer on what God wants to plant and nurture in us today.

We simply can't move forward while we are looking back. I believe Jesus wants us to deal with the past – the issues that still 'press our buttons'. As we surrender our past hurts to him we give him 'permission' to heal and restore us. Let's not hold on to past bitterness so that it corrupts and infects us throughout our lives. 'Let go and let God' is a popular saying: but it's powerful.

PAUSE FOR THOUGHT
Do you often revisit the past? If so, is it a pleasant or painful experience? Is anything from the past defining how you live today?

WATCH: 23:40-25:50
In this moving clip, we see how Ebenezer's sister, Fan, has apparently consistently asked their father, a hard man, to let his son come home and he has, at last, agreed. The depth of the alienated Ebenezer's love for her is obvious. As long as she lives, says Fan, her brother will never be lonely again …

Fan tries to persuade her brother to forgive their father and forget past hurts.

It becomes clear that his father's attitude has come about because he hadn't forgiven his son for the fact that his mother died giving birth to him. Fan died after giving birth to her son, too. It seems Scrooge has never forgiven him, either.

THINK ABOUT

We sometimes hold grudges against people when actually, whatever happened isn't their fault directly. We may have family feuds and not really know the reason why – perhaps there was a problem many years ago, the cause long-forgotten. On the other hand, the cause might be all-too well-remembered! We mull it over, feed the memory and are quick to recall the details before others.

Young Scrooge has suffered intensely for something that wasn't his fault. Yet, he repeats the cycle. He loved Fan so much that when she died after having Fred, he blamed the child.

Bitterness is deadly. It colours a whole life. You may know people who have been unable to move on from something that has happened to them. They seem to have stopped at a certain point in time – a time when they were terribly hurt, maybe even back in childhood; they have grown in age and experience, and yet something is stunted within them.

Forgiveness is a great key to moving on. If we don't forgive, we remain locked into that situation or person who hurt us. If you're asking yourself, 'Why should I forgive? Why should I let them off the hook?' remember, forgiving is letting *us* off the hook – the life-destroying hook of bitterness.

PAUSE FOR THOUGHT
In the story of the unforgiving servant in Matthew 18:21-35, it seems that Jesus is teaching that if we don't forgive, we can remain in a kind of tormenting prison. I don't want to be there: do you?

WATCH: 25:53-28:16

Scrooge next finds himself viewing a party. It's the Fezziwigs' celebrations. Mr Fezziwig, to whom he was apprenticed, was a kind soul. He appears to have given a great deal of happiness to all who knew him. The ghost points out that the party didn't cost much; why then is Scrooge so full of praise for Fezziwig? Scrooge blurts out the truth – that it wasn't about the money; and he seems, for a moment, remorseful, as he remembers Bob Cratchit, his clerk who, of course, he has not treated with any kind of generosity.

In this clip we also see Scrooge in love with Alice, who is poor. He declares he will always love her ...

THINK ABOUT

The happiness of the young Ebenezer here is such a contrast to what he becomes.

People change. Feelings change. Scrooge's feelings towards Alice, as we see later in the film, do indeed alter, as his priorities shift. Like Scrooge, we can lose our way in life; it can happen fast, or sometimes very slowly. Our minds can wander from the things of God as 'the world' and its values subtly take over. Playing sport, working hard, music, relationships – there's nothing wrong in any of these; but when something (or someone) begins to take priority over our devotion to God, we can begin to veer off course. We can, in effect, lose our 'first love' (Revelation 2:4).

If we love Jesus, he has to be before everything else in our lives – he demands nothing less. That doesn't mean we can't enjoy other things, but he has to take precedence.

> PAUSE FOR THOUGHT
> In Luke 14:26, Jesus uses hyperbole to teach that we need to love him more than anyone else – indeed, even more than our own lives. If we don't, then we can't be his disciples. How does that challenge you today?

WATCH: 28:22-35:36

Here we see how Scrooge begins the unhappy descent into who he later becomes. Fezziwig's views on life are very different to those of Mr Jorkin, representing corporate power, and he won't sell out.

The greatest blow for Ebenezer happens as his sister dies. She asks him to take care of her child, but he has left the room. As he watches the death scene played out before him, he cries out for her forgiveness in a very emotive scene.

Then we see that he has left Mr Fezziwig's and has taken a position as a clerk with the heavily materialistic and ambitious Mr Jorkin. Here Ebenezer meets Jacob Marley. In their initial conversation we can see what appears to be a meeting of minds. Marley is quick to share his views on the changing nature of the times – some of which, he believes, will be 'violent'. At this point Scrooge is understandably feeling the world is becoming a harsh place. He thinks one has to 'steel oneself' in order to survive, and to escape being 'crushed under with the weak and the infirm'.

Later, does Scrooge have a moment of regret over what has happened to Fezziwig? No matter; his path is set.

THINK ABOUT

I think this section of the film is the saddest because we can see how Scrooge is setting his feet on a path that will only lead him downwards, away from any happiness. He has put walls up to avoid being hurt again; but when we build walls, we run the risk of becoming the prisoner inside.

Truly, the world has been unkind to Scrooge. However, teaming up with like-minded Marley will do him no good. Proverbs 12:26 tells us that we need to choose our friends with care, because if we don't, we can be led astray. Who do we have in our lives that will build us up, encourage us and help us follow Jesus more closely?

I love the story of David and Jonathan in 1 Samuel. This biblical account is often offered as an example of what true friendship should be like. Jonathan, apart from being a godly man and brave warrior, was a terrific encourager. He was loyal to his friend (and interestingly, to his father, Saul, too, dying alongside him in battle), behaving in an almost inexplicably self-sacrificial way. He realised that David was God's chosen successor to his father, rather than himself, but he didn't seem to let that fact cause him any resentment. Actually, we can see in Jonathan a 'type' of Jesus – the one who covers us with his own robe of righteousness (1 Samuel 18:4; 1 Corinthians 1:30). Jesus is the greatest friend of all (John 15:14-16) and, like the best of friends, I think he is looking for ways to build us up, encourage us; reasons to say 'well done'. Likewise, we should be keen to do the same for others.

Let's make sure we cultivate friendships in which we can affirm each other. One of the things a good friend does is *listen*. Sometimes we want to jump in with all sorts of remarks, comments about our own lives, and advice, but to really listen, and to ensure the other person knows they have been heard, and therefore valued, is a great gift. Real friends also challenge us. To allow them to do this, we need to know that they love us. I have friends who I can trust not to always flatter me; they'll offer their honest opinions! Such gentle challenge doesn't affect the friendship negatively; actually, it strengthens it because I know I can trust them to tell me the truth. Sometimes I need nudging in my attitudes and life, and I am grateful for the candid contribution of friends who care.

PAUSE FOR THOUGHT
Do you have some good friends you can be 'real' with? Are you the kind of friend who listens, and who people can trust to tell them 'the truth in love' (Ephesians 4:15)?

WATCH: 35:37-38:05

In this scene we see the devastating effect on relationships caused by a heart hardened as a response to life's cruel blows. I think it especially poignant that Alice tells Scrooge that he is in fear of the world. Fear of further hurt can surely turn a heart cold as it seeks out ways in which to protect itself.

Alice is releasing Scrooge from his promise to marry her; his attitude in regard to the world has changed, and consequently he has changed towards her too. Ruthless ambition has taken root. Alice tells Ebenezer that an idol of gold has replaced her in his heart: the idol of materialism, as he relentlessly pursues wealth. She wishes him happiness in the life he has chosen … a deeply ironic statement.

THINK ABOUT

We may not have control over the things that happen to us, but we do have a choice about how we respond to them.

I have a friend who lives with a life-limiting illness. As she has grown closer to Jesus, she has gradually become more filled with peace, and a great love for the Lord. She could be filled with resentment but she's not. As a result, she is an inspiration to be around.

When I think back to the time when I had a serious illness, exacerbated by severe agoraphobia, I could be bitter that for so long, I was unable to live a 'normal' life. My mum was a great support to me during that time, but later she became ill and at the time of writing has many health difficulties including vascular dementia and Parkinson's disease. So I can't really share the joy of my todays with her. But I also know that one day we will both be with Jesus, happily reunited – not remembering the sad things, the pain, the grief (Revelation 21:4).

It's all about focus: we can let suffering twist our view of life, or we can raise our eyes and look to Jesus, remembering that he didn't say we would have an easy life (John 16:33) but he did tell us he'd be in it with us (Matthew 28:20). This world is full of uncertainties, but we aren't to live in fear; fear, when we let it control us, can have a devastating effect on us. 1 John 4:18 tells us that when we know perfect love, fear must flee – and that perfect love is found in the God who sent his Son to us. Neither are we meant to have 'idols' – anything that takes the place of Jesus. After all, what good will our idol be on the day Jesus calls us to be with him? Think about the story of the rich ruler in Matthew 19. His idol stopped him following Jesus whole-heartedly. What, if anything, stops us?

PAUSE FOR THOUGHT
Has anything replaced Jesus in your heart? Talk to your God about this now.

WATCH: 44:30–47:30
The deathbed scene of Jacob Marley is very telling.

The ambitious and manipulative Mr Jorkin has been discovered as an embezzler, at which point Marley and Scrooge offered to save the company by making good from their private resources on what Jorkin had embezzled – on condition that they could buy further company shares, thereby owning 51 per cent of it.

In the first part of this clip, we fast-forward to where Marley is dying, on Christmas Eve (although Scrooge won't visit him till his business is done; his bedside manner is also very brusque!). Marley seems to have had a revelation about his business dealings – and about life in general. He says to Scrooge that they were wrong. He tells Scrooge that while there's still time, he should save himself. Scrooge asks, rather impatiently, what from?

The end of the clip contains a very good summary of what Scrooge has become.

THINK ABOUT

'Money is the root of all evil' is a popular maxim, but actually, 1 Timothy 6:10 says: 'For the *love* of money is a root of all kinds of evil. Some people, eager for money, have wandered from the faith and pierced themselves with many griefs' (my emphasis). Material blessing can be used to bless others, as we eventually see in the story of Scrooge. But *loving* money above all else – that's another matter.

There are those who believe this world is all there is. Some of us may ask, with Scrooge, what we need to be saved from! Is there really a 'judgement' for the way we have lived; an eternal separation for those who haven't wanted to live in relationship with their Creator on earth? Or is there a kind of fuzzy warm place called 'heaven' where everyone will go, regardless of belief, where we will all play harps and sit on clouds? A study of the teachings of Jesus should give us all the clues we need.

Right back in Genesis 3, humankind turned its back on the Creator and that was when sin and separation from God entered the world. Romans 6:23 warns us: 'the wages of sin is death', so clearly we need to be saved from the consequences of our human rebellion. But how can we be reconciled to God? Marley talks about 'saving yourself' but the Bible makes it clear we can't do that. Our salvation, our being made right with God, is his gift! The second part of the Romans quote tells us so. We can't 'save ourselves' at all.

Perhaps there's something in humanity that makes us feel we should be 'doing' something to earn our salvation – religious works, maybe. But however good our 'works' might be, they can't make us right with God (Isaiah 64:6). God is sinless perfection; nothing we can do can make us 'good enough' to dwell in his presence.

We need to call out to the One who offers us life. Jesus promised paradise to the thief on the cross, who was in no position to save himself (Luke 23:43). If Jacob Marley was a real person, and had called to Jesus on his deathbed when he realised he'd lived wrong and needed saving, then surely Jesus would not have turned him away.

When his friend Lazarus died, Jesus told

Lazarus' sister Martha, 'I am the resurrection and the life. The one who believes in me will live, even though they die; and whoever lives by believing in me will never die' (John 11:25). How we consider this will depend on how we view the character of Jesus. Who was he? Was he really who he claimed to be?

PAUSE FOR THOUGHT

If Jesus really was the Messiah, the Son of God, God in the flesh, who came to redeem us, make us right with God, then his words are worth listening to. He claimed to be 'the life' in John 14:6 – see also John 1:4, where we read that life was 'in him'. What does that mean? What significance does it have for me, and for you, in the light of eternity?

ADVENT CONNECTION

Read: Isaiah 9:6-7

> For to us a child is born,
> to us a son is given,
> and the government will be on his shoulders.

And he will be called
Wonderful Counsellor, Mighty God,
Everlasting Father, Prince of Peace.
Of the greatness of his government and peace
there will be no end.
He will reign on David's throne …

Long before Jesus arrived, he was expected. Deuteronomy 18:18 God speaks of a prophet like Moses who would come, and it is clear that by Jesus' time the arrival of the Messiah, or Anointed One, was anticipated (see John 1:25,41; 4:25). From the line of David (Isaiah 11:1), this Bethlehem-born figure 'whose origins are from old' would rule his people, be their shepherd (Micah 5:2 – see also Matthew 2:6), ushering in a time of peace and prosperity.

The Old Testament is filled with pointers to the Messiah, the Saviour. The Gospel of Matthew is very interesting in that respect. Matthew 1 tells us that 'All this took place to fulfil what the Lord had said through the prophet: "The virgin will conceive and give birth to a son, and they will call him Immanuel" (which means "God with us")' – a reference to Isaiah 7:14. In Matthew 2 we read that King Herod himself was well aware of a coming Messiah who would clearly threaten his own rule. Even that the infant Jesus would escape the grip of the murderous Herod is foretold in Scripture (Matthew 2:13-15). Take a look, when you have the time, at Matthew 4:12-20 (Isaiah 9:2), Zechariah 9:9, Psalm 22 and Isaiah 53.

Under oppressive Roman occupation, we can imagine how the Jewish people were longing for their Messiah to come. But was Jesus really the long-awaited figure? He certainly seemed to carry out the miracles expected by the coming King – messianic 'signs', as we see in the Gospel of John. So, was he going to crush the Romans to set captive Israel free? No wonder the authorities were so worried! A messianic figure could cause untold problems for the people. John 11:48-50 shows us plainly how the Jewish rulers of the time were thinking; they were deeply concerned that if Jesus continued in his popular ministry, it would have serious consequences in regard to the Roman occupiers of their nation. The high priest's remark is especially revealing: 'You do not realise that it is better … that one man die for the people than that the whole nation perish.' These words were prophetic indeed.

Looking back to the start of Jesus' ministry, he went to his hometown of Nazareth and in the synagogue, read from the book of Isaiah – clearly making the messianic claim:

> The Spirit of the Lord is on me,
> because he has anointed me
> to proclaim good news to the poor.
> He has sent me to proclaim freedom for the
>   prisoners
> and recovery of sight for the blind,
> to set the oppressed free, to proclaim the year of
>   the Lord's favour.
> … Today this scripture is fulfilled in your hearing.
>   (Luke 4:18, 19, 21; see Isaiah 61:1-2)

While he actually fulfilled his messianic 'brief', things didn't turn out the way people expected. All through Jesus' ministry, people queried his credentials. Wasn't this man the son of Joseph, the local carpenter (Mark 6:3; Luke 4:22)? How could this be the Messiah? And why – although clearly fulfilling another messianic expectation in Matthew 21:4-6, when riding into Jerusalem – did he allow himself to be beaten and murdered there? Wasn't he supposed to save Israel from their oppressors?

Have you noticed that God doesn't always act in ways we expect? Or in *people* we might readily accept? Jesus' own disciples didn't 'get it', even after the resurrection (Acts 1:6). And Simon Peter's high point of faith in Matthew 16:16, when he declared that Jesus was the Messiah, the Son of God, was followed by a complete misunderstanding of Jesus' mission (vv. 22-23).

Jesus' origins are eternal. Immanuel, God in the flesh (John 1:1-3; Colossians 2:9; Hebrews 1:3). John 1:1-18 makes excellent reading, especially at Christmastime. The Creator himself came into the world but people didn't recognise him. Yet, 'he gave the right to become children of God' to all who believed in him. The promised and awaited one came to live among us; he made God known. The first Advent. Fully man, he entered into what it means to be human; fully God, he showed us what God is like. Only a perfect man could lay down his life on behalf of fallen humankind; only God could live a life of sinless perfection and offer it as a sacrifice of infinite worth.

Israel looked into the past and saw they were promised a redeemer. We can look into the past and see how Jesus fulfilled the prophecies. Studying his life in the light of Old Testament promises is an awesome revelation.

PAUSE FOR THOUGHT
- Do you need to come to Jesus for counsel and guidance today? Do you need his peace?

- Do you struggle with understanding how Jesus could be 'God in a body' – in effect, 'gave God a face'? Why do you think it is important for us to see that Jesus really is fully God and fully man? How should believing this is true affect our view of God, and ourselves?
- Do you need to be set free from 'a prison'? Are you unable to 'see' in some area? Do you feel 'oppressed'? Look at 1 Peter 5:7 and spend a few moments telling Jesus your worries.

ACTIVITY SUGGESTIONS

- Imagine your life as a garden. What good things do you feel God is planting? Is there anything from your past which threatens to distort or destroy these things? If it helps, write down your thoughts and bring them to God, one by one.
- Read the Lord's Prayer in Matthew 6:9-13. Read on to verses 14 and 15, which also talk about forgiveness. Do you need to forgive someone? What can you do to move forward in forgiveness – or to encourage a friend to do so?

REFLECTION

The film so far has been very much rooted in the darkness of wrong choices. Reflect on some of your good choices. Did you pray before you made them? Review your day (now or later, depending on when you are reading this!). Is there anything you have thought, said, or done that you know your friend Jesus is pleased with? Can you imagine him encouraging you with a 'well done'?

PRAYER

Lord, help me to live for you, learning from what has gone before, but walking in the freedom you bring. You are the Lord of life, the long-awaited Messiah who came to save us. Thank you for the eternal life you promise – that life which is connected with you who are Life itself. Thank you for your goodness and your love. Amen.

CHAPTER THREE
LIVING NOW

PREPARE YOURSELF

Think of ways in which you encounter the peaceful presence of God. Is it through prayer? Worship? Alone, in the quietness of solitude? What can you do to ensure you have these regular times, after Christmas is over and the New Year begins? If you feel you don't encounter God anywhere, be honest. Would you like to, this Christmas?

TO START

We're so often caught up in the past or are so busy thinking about what's going to happen next that we miss what's going on today. Yet God has given us the incredible gift of 'now': the 'present' of the present!

For a long while I was unable to go anywhere due to the effects of illness and subsequent agoraphobia. One day I was well enough to sit in the garden. It was early on in the year, and I suddenly saw a very small flower. That I could even see it – having suffered from Ménière's disease, which takes away balance, hearing, even eyesight as things spin uncontrollably – was a miracle to me. Now, I would probably pull that 'flower' up as a weed! However, having been through that illness, I appreciate the moments of my life more than I did before. Having lost some of the hearing in my right ear, I especially appreciate birdsong. I love the dawn chorus, the call of a tawny owl, a solitary blackbird singing.

We waste so much time focusing on things we can do nothing about. We can't change what happened in the past, only our attitude of today. We also have no control over the future, even though we sometimes think we do – ask anyone who has lost a job, a pension plan, suffered an untimely death or chronic long-term sickness of a loved one, divorce, or developed a life-changing illness.

Mark 8:36 challenges us: 'What good is it for someone to gain the whole world, yet forfeit their soul?' It's a case of perspective. While we need to be responsible and make wise choices, we can spend so much time concentrating on 'the future' that we miss the small, wonderful things today offers, and the gratitude of the moment.

Let's not miss the gift of life that God has given us right now. As we begin to consider

Scrooge and his next supernatural encounter, this time with the Spirit of Christmas Present, let's keep in mind that *this* is the time when we are alive to enjoy God's presence. We are living *now*.

PAUSE FOR THOUGHT

Spend a moment thanking God for your life, your breath, the people you love, the blue (or grey!) sky, the snow, the rain, the sunshine; Christmas blessings and the hope of a new year; the fact that winter always turns to spring. We're alive! Praise God.

WATCH: 48:35-50:00

Scrooge now encounters a very different spirit – this one, to me, is seriously scary! A chuckling, lavish, over-the-top Father Christmas character.

Ebenezer begins to complain that he's too old to change. In essence, why not target someone else for redemption – someone younger!

This clip is interesting because Jesus is mentioned. Christmas isn't about how we live just one day of the year. The spirit talks about the Christmas child, who lives in people's hearts. Scrooge hasn't chosen to seek him in his heart;

so he will seek him in other people's hearts. We are transported with Ebenezer to a community of miners, who are singing *Hark! the Herald Angels Sing*. The message is clear: sometimes the poor are richer than the rich; something we will consider further a little later in this chapter.

THINK ABOUT

There's so much to consider in this clip! There's the question of age. When Scrooge whines about being too old, it reminds me of the elderly Moses asking God to send someone else to carry out his will, in Exodus 4:13! But the truth is, no one is beyond God's redemption, or his calling – however old, however young, however far away from God we might think we are.

In Matthew 5:3 Jesus tells us: 'Blessed are the poor in spirit, for theirs is the kingdom of heaven.' I wonder how you read that phrase, 'poor in spirit'. Not necessarily materially poor, perhaps – this doesn't automatically equate with godliness, as I'm sure we are aware. In Proverbs 30:8-9 the writer pleads with God to give him just enough for the day, because he fears that if he has too much he may turn away from God, but if he became poor, he could be tempted into theft.

Age or infirmity might limit some of us in what we feel we can 'do' for the Lord, but I learned long ago that although God appears to have many people who want to 'work' for him, he doesn't have so many who just want to simply 'be' with him. Whatever our age and circumstances, surely we can all find time to 'be'? When I was first ill I remember saying to God, 'All I wanted was to work for you,' and his gentle reply, 'I don't want you to work for me. I want to do my work in and through you.'

As believers, our 'works' should flow from a constant connection to the Life – that is, Jesus. He challenges us, in the Upper Room Discourse, that we need to remain in him if we want to bear fruit (John 15:4). How do we remain in him? He makes that clear: obey him. How do we obey? We must love each other (vv. 10-12). As we remain in him, his life flows through us and out to others. If we look elsewhere, to the past, to the future, and perhaps allow regret or anxiety to fudge our thinking, we aren't living fully in the 'now' of God, in constant communion with the One who loves us best; and we may miss opportunities to listen to him as he speaks to us about the person in front of us, wherever we are, so giving us the opportunity to pray for them, or to bless them in some other way.

As we remain in Jesus, the Spirit of God, who lives in our hearts when we come to Jesus as our Lord and Saviour, begins to produce his fruit within us – the 'love, joy, peace, forbearance, kindness, goodness, faithfulness, gentleness and self-control' that we read of in Galatians 5:22-23. We can't work these things up. They are things of God, evident in us as we surrender to his love and will.

PAUSE FOR THOUGHT
Do you tend to 'work' for Jesus, rather than 'be' with him? Why is that? Spend a few moments thinking about it.

WATCH: 51:00-53:55
It's Christmas Day in the poor but happy Cratchit household. Bob and Tiny Tim have been to church, and Bob talks about Tim's rather optimistic reflections on how seeing him, people might be reminded of the One who healed the sick.

It seems that Tiny Tim will not live – the spirit has foreseen it. Scrooge appears to feel some compassion, but his words about decreasing 'the surplus population' are fired at him like arrows that clearly hit the mark.

THINK ABOUT
I wonder if the people in Tim's world really did find it 'pleasant' to be reminded of Jesus on

Christmas Day by seeing a boy who couldn't walk. This part made me think about how we, as Christians, view sickness generally.

Jesus had a ministry of healing the sick and setting people free from darkness. As we have already seen, the wonders he was performing pointed to who he really was: they were 'signs', as John's Gospel asserts (e.g. John 2:23). He also said that his followers would see the sick healed (Mark 16:17-18). Perhaps you know of someone who has been miraculously restored to health?

I had oral thrush when I was younger. One evening, at a celebration meeting, we were asked to praise Jesus out loud – not something I did in those days, in public! But as I began to worship, I was filled with the Holy Spirit, and the condition in my mouth was healed and never returned. I went on to develop another illness later, which I have mentioned earlier. That wasn't something that was healed straight away, although the Lord did wonderfully restore my health after some difficult years. I also know people who are living close to God who have not as yet experienced full healing – as you may do too.

I think we have to be careful when talking to people who aren't yet healed from their infirmities. It can be very disheartening when we are sick, to have veiled suggestions (or sometimes not so veiled!) that we may somehow be lacking in faith – or in sin! So let's walk in sensitivity and discernment with our friends and loved ones who are unwell, praying that God may restore them not only in body, but in mind, soul and spirit too.

I have seen physical and emotional health improve as a person forgives themselves and others; but more, a beauty of spirit appearing, even if bodily health hasn't yet been fully restored. This whole area of healing, sickness and suffering is a mystery – while praying in faith and obedience, we also need to be careful not to judge.

PAUSE FOR THOUGHT
Isaiah 53:5 tells us that 'by his [Jesus'] wounds we are healed'. Spend a few moments in reflection. How does that verse speak to you today?

WATCH: 53:55-57:06
Now we are at the Cratchits' Christmas table. The Cratchits – particularly Mrs Cratchit – reluctantly toast Scrooge. Bob Cratchit seems such a forgiving man, very magnanimous in

his attitude. Then, switching scenes, we see that Scrooge's nephew, Fred, is also keen to toast him, and realistically points out that the only person who is really suffering from Scrooge's miserable demeanour is himself!

THINK ABOUT

Our selfishness can hurt others, but it hurts us too. Scrooge may be rich in the eyes of the world, but actually he is poor – as we can see by the way the loveless and unlovely man lives. In Revelation 3:17-18, Jesus speaks to the Church in Laodicea of a similar poverty; they think they're rich but they don't realise they are 'poor, blind and naked'.

Jesus, not 'acquired wealth', is the answer to the inner emptiness we often try to fill with accumulated 'stuff'. True fulfilment, filling that 'inner empty', as Scrooge eventually finds out, is not found in the misery of selfish living, or the obsessive acquiring of material wealth.

The paradox here is that the kind-hearted Bob Cratchit and Fred are the ones Scrooge has been most unpleasant to, yet they are both willing to bless. Blessing someone we don't like or who has hurt us isn't easy. In Luke 6:28 Jesus said we should 'bless those who curse [us], [and] pray for those who ill-treat [us]'. Romans 12:14 goes on to say that we should bless and not curse. In this way, we are loving our enemies. But why should we?

Well, a reading of Matthew 5:43-48 tells us. So 'that you may be children of your Father in heaven'. Sometimes we need to remind ourselves how gracious and forgiving God has been to us. We, as his children, should be like our Father. To do good to our enemies marks us out as very different to the world. It's actually quite hard to keep on being angry with someone when we are praying for them on a regular basis, so we might find it very freeing!

PAUSE FOR THOUGHT
Think about someone you may not consider 'a friend'. Ask God how he would like you to pray for that person.

WATCH: 57:07-59:24

In this scene, scripture is being read out in the poorhouse: the 'love chapter', 1 Corinthians 13, which is often read at weddings. This famous passage speaks so honestly about how if we don't have love, we have nothing.

Scrooge's former sweetheart, Alice, is working among the poor, making a difference with her kindness. How bitter for Scrooge, watching her, but cut off from her love.

Then the Spirit of Christmas Present shows Ebenezer two children, hidden under his cloak. They represent ignorance and want. Ignorance in particular is dangerous – how true that is. At this point in the film, Scrooge is beginning to really see his own ignorance about the suffering of people. Can no one help them? His own words come back to haunt him once more: 'Are there no prisons, are there no workhouses?'

THINK ABOUT

In the busyness of our world, we can often forget the plight of people less well-off than ourselves. We may even become almost immune to the suffering of others, especially when we are watching appeals on TV about people in other countries.

Sometimes, though, suffering that seems 'far away' or rather impersonal can draw near. We might visit another country on holiday, for example, or speak with people who have come to live in our own towns and cities, who have known what it is like to flee persecution, war, starvation and other hardships. When we listen to them, we may begin to realise that those we see or read about whose lives seem so far from our own comparatively comfortable situations, are *real* people with real stories, just like us, who have been caught in poverty, war zones, trafficking. Do I choose to live in ignorance? Maybe my busy life just hasn't got room for the suffering of others. It's someone else's problem; isn't it?

Scrooge was learning the lesson that actually, no, it's everyone's problem.

At this time of year, it is all the more distressing to see people sleeping in shop doorways. We can become cynical about this if we aren't careful. I remember doing some street evangelism on Saturday nights in a large town. I met many homeless people at that time, some with surprising stories – people who had been financially successful and had had a personal tragedy they couldn't cope with, and they'd eventually lost everything. It altered my perception of what it means to be homeless.

PAUSE FOR THOUGHT

Do you have a homeless shelter nearby, or some other charity that is working in an area of need that you would like to be involved with? Think about what you may be able to do to support them, practically or in prayer, after Christmas.

ADVENT CONNECTION

Read: Luke 2:8-18

> And there were shepherds living out in the fields near by, keeping watch over their flocks at night. An angel of the Lord appeared to them … and they were terrified. But the angel said to them, 'Do not be afraid. I bring you good news that will cause great joy for all the people. Today … a Saviour has been born to you; he is the Messiah, the Lord. … Suddenly a great company of the heavenly host appeared with the angel, praising God and saying,
>
> 'Glory to God in the highest heaven, and on earth peace to those on whom his favour rests.'

Christmas really wouldn't be complete without the angels and the shepherds, a staple for every nativity play. It's really sweet to see small shepherds wearing old tea towels on their heads, clutching toy sheep and warbling *Away in a Manger*, isn't it? However, we may forget that the original shepherds were far from 'sweet'; they were pretty much *persona non grata* back in the days and culture into which Jesus was born. They were not desirable company. But just as in his later ministry Jesus would reach out to those who weren't acceptable, at his birth it was the unacceptable who saw him first.

These shepherds were just living out their ordinary, day-to-day routine when all of a sudden, they had a supernatural experience that changed their lives. Unlike the fictional Scrooge, this was a real encounter with heavenly beings, resulting in the shepherds' 'meeting' the (very) young Son of God – the One who had come to bring peace between God and humankind.

Whatever they had thought before, whatever people had said about them, perhaps judged them, none of that would have mattered in the immediacy of their 'now' experience of heavenly reality. Their perception of themselves would surely have been turned upside down – God had chosen *them* to welcome the Messiah! How it affected their lives from then on is difficult to judge; although it's interesting to see that they 'spread the word' of their experience – evangelism springing from encounter.

People who have extraordinary experiences of encountering Jesus are often to be found in the most unexpected places. I have met and worked with those who had a real encounter with Jesus in prison, for instance. You yourself might have met Jesus in the most surprising way, and in one radical moment, your 'now' experience of him has changed how you view yourself, your life and your future.

I met Jesus one July afternoon when I was struggling to cope after a series of difficulties had caused shockwaves in my life. In the middle of all my angst, my granny came to stay. I'd loved listening to her stories of Jesus when I was a kid, but now I was older, holding quite a lot of anger, I wasn't so keen. Still, I drove her to the local Christian book shop and while browsing discovered a book about someone who had a personal relationship with Jesus. It was then that I realised it was possible to truly 'know him'. Some time later, at home, I got down on my knees. I said, 'If you're really there, Jesus, will you handle my life? Because I can't handle it anymore.' I didn't hear an angelic choir, but I did discover a peace that I hadn't had before.

So, I started my walk with Jesus. I found a church where I really felt his presence, and began to learn more of him; I got baptised and filled with the Holy Spirit, and started Bible college extension studies with a view to 'working full-time for God'. Then, I became very ill and couldn't do anything at all. My physical health improved in time but I still had life-curtailing agoraphobia and didn't know how I was going to make a living. Then, I had an encounter with the Holy Spirit, after which I didn't ask for work;

I just praised God. This went on for nine days. On the ninth day, a phone call out of the blue changed everything, when someone asked me to edit a book. From that time to this – nearly twenty years later – God has graciously provided me with a full-time job as a freelance writer and editor of Christian books and magazines. I have seen his hand in all sorts of ways, providing and supporting me through good times and bad.

God is a God of miracles – small ones, big ones. Unlike the shepherds, we may not get to see a visible sign or hear audible words. But when he sent his Son into the world it was for the greatest miracle of all: that he could tear down the barrier between God and humanity, shedding his blood on the cross for you and me.

The Messiah, the Saviour, has come, and because our extraordinary God has broken into our ordinary lives, we can 'live different' today.

PAUSE FOR THOUGHT
- Have you ever felt 'unacceptable'? How does it feel to know that the shepherds, some of society's outcasts, were the first to be invited to meet Jesus?
- How might encountering God in the

'now' affect the way we think about our past, our present, and our future?

- Do you have a testimony of meeting Jesus? Has the experience changed the way you view yourself – your life? Why not ask God for an opportunity to share this with someone?

ACTIVITY SUGGESTIONS

- Sometimes, when life is especially stressful or tough, the last thing we are experiencing is God's peaceful presence! Spend some time considering the words of Psalm 46:10, which encourages us to 'Be still, and know that I am God'. There are essentially two parts to this – the part that God requires of us: 'Be still', and the reason for our stillness: who he is. Meditate on how the two parts connect. He is God. We need to be still before him. Or perhaps simply 'be'.

- Go for a short walk in the park or the countryside, or step out into your garden. (Wrap up warmly!)If that's not possible, sit quietly in your room, by a window if you can. What do you see, hear, feel, touch, experience in this moment that lifts your heart and that you feel grateful f or?

REFLECTION

What prevents you from living in the moment? Try to be fully present to enjoy the festivities, rather than giving in to worry about whether or not the turkey will be too dry/too small, or the table decorations aren't 'Christmassy' enough! One of the ways to stay 'in the now' is to be intentionally thankful for the moment. How can you factor in thankfulness this Advent season?

PRAYER

Father, I thank you for everything you have done for me. Thank you that you love me, that I can encounter you, and experience your peace. I especially thank you for [name something or someone]. Thank you that you care for the sick, the outcast, those who others think are unlovely. Help me not to close my eyes to need, but to be your hands and feet where you would send me. Amen.

CHAPTER FOUR

FUTURE ... PERFECT?

PREPARE YOURSELF

Christmas Day is edging ever closer, so you may want to dip in and out of this chapter as time allows! Read out loud, slowly, Matthew 6:25-34. If you haven't the time, just read verse 34:

> Therefore do not worry about tomorrow, for tomorrow will worry about itself. Each day has enough trouble of its own.

This is especially true of the Christmas season, I find! Now read verse 33, about seeking 'first his kingdom and his righteousness'. What does Jesus promise us, if we do this? What do you believe Jesus might be saying to you, as the 'big day' draws near?

TO START

Can we change the future? In this film, it seems so! The Bible, with its prophecies, appears to teach that some things will certainly happen; the

One who is the 'Beginning and the End' knows all things that are and will be (Revelation 21:6). We have already seen that God had a plan for his Messiah. So, what of the individual and their circumstances?

It is true that what we do today will affect our tomorrows. The choices we make both in our actions, and in our reactions to things that are outside our control are based in the free will I believe God has given us. We don't *have* to act defensively when someone unintentionally offends us. We don't *have* to respond to that trigger when something is said that reminds us of how we were treated in the past.

1 Corinthians 2:16 tells us we 'have the mind of Christ'. With the Holy Spirit's help, we can choose to think differently. What we think will affect our actions, and our actions will affect our lives. Jeremiah 29:11 assures us that God has a good plan for us – whether we decide to surrender to his will, though, is our choice. It may be helpful to view our lives in terms of a jigsaw puzzle. We don't see the big picture, and often spend a lot of time hammering in pieces that just won't fit – possibly because they aren't actually part of our picture! In fact, they might be part of somebody else's picture. Think about it! Isn't it better to cooperate with the One who made the puzzle that is you, in the first place?

Now we see how Scrooge's future will turn out if he doesn't change his ways. It's all very well to mentally acknowledge what may happen to us if we don't alter our behaviours, but it is another thing entirely to see the future consequences of our actions – as Scrooge discovers. And in the end, we witness the happy results of a penitent heart.

PAUSE FOR THOUGHT
Before you watch these clips/read the comments, ask God to show you if there is anything in your life he would like you to change for your future well-being (and for the happiness of those around you).

WATCH: 59:26-1:03:13

ow encounters his final spirit – the Spirit of Christmas Yet to Come. Unlike the others, it is silent, and therefore much more intimidating. He is more afraid of it than any of the others – hardly surprising. The future is a mysterious country, potentially terrifying in its silence as, unknown, it cannot speak to us. Scrooge, having seen the past and the present, is in fear of what is to come. So, here is the future, played out for him, if he doesn't change his ways. Is he *really* too old to change? Are any of us? Not that he doesn't repent of his actions … but of course, repentance means transformation, or else it isn't true repentance.

The first thing we see is that Tiny Tim has passed away. His brother, Peter, is reading Psalm 91 and the weight of grief and sadness lies heavily upon the Cratchit family.

THINK ABOUT

When I was about fourteen, I was going through a hard time at school. One day I picked up a King James Version of the New Testament and Psalms. I found it hard to understand, being written in what I thought of as 'Shakespearean' English. (I was relieved to find out later that God also spoke to us in modern-day language, once I bought a copy of the NIV!) But I turned to Psalm 91 – not knowing the Bible at all – and comforting words jumped out at me. As I read this psalm, full of God's love and protection, I knew that he was real. The journey towards discipleship probably started right there, although it would be more than ten years before I submitted to Jesus and began the adventure of knowing him.

There are so many places in the Bible where we are told not to be fearful. Indeed, the angelic visitors who appeared to Mary, and the shepherds, were swift to say 'don't be afraid'. The enemy deals in fear. Anxiety is one of the weapons he wields to get our eyes off Jesus and onto situations and circumstances. It's no surprise that so many people struggle with fear in all of its manifestations. I have found that one of the great antidotes to anxiety is to thank and praise God. It refocuses me as I declare truths about who God is: he is on my side, he is greater than the enemy, he loves me. He is God most high – the Creator of all. The redeemer. My friend. Father God sent his Son to save me. When trouble or hardship or grief or loss arrive at my door, still nothing can separate me from his love (Romans 8:38-39). He is Lord. I'm sure you can think of many wonderful characteristics of our loving Creator to speak out loud when you are feeling afraid.

PAUSE FOR THOUGHT
Think about your favourite psalm. Why do you like it? In what way does God speak to you in and through it?

WATCH: 1:03:15-1:07:52; 1:07:52-1:09; 1:09-1:10:49

In the first scene, we are watching the undertaker, laundress and Scrooge's charwoman bringing his belongings to the pawnbroker – even the bed curtains and blankets. In the second clip, the wealthy businessman says the only reason he will go Scrooge's funeral is if there's free food!

What a contrast to the sadness of Tiny Tim's death. Tim has been loved, and is missed, but Scrooge has died alone, not prepared at all for eternity. There's no love; no one will mourn for Ebenezer. The money he worshipped has been left to his company. What a futile, wasted life!

Actually, at this point, Scrooge doesn't realise it is he who has died. But, in the third clip, he realises that he is, indeed, the deceased – the person who has had his belongings picked over by those who don't care; whose funeral people don't want to attend unless there's something in it for them. Seeing his grave, with an anguished wail, his repentance seems genuine, and raw. Surely the future can change, if he changes? He wants to 'make good the wrongs' of his life!

THINK ABOUT

Someone who made good the wrongs he had committed, not through fear of the future, but because he was accepted by Jesus, was Zacchaeus.

We read his story in Luke 19:1-10. Zacchaeus was less than popular among the Jewish people. He was well-off – working for the Romans as a chief tax collector, a collaborator – and he was also dishonest in his dealings.

In the Gospel account, Jesus invites himself to Zacchaeus' home, and is welcomed there. The people around Jesus aren't too impressed, though; why would he go to visit someone so unworthy – such a 'sinner'? But Zacchaeus has a heart change through meeting Jesus. Verse 8 tells us he offers to give half of his possessions away to poor people, and to generously reimburse those he has cheated. True repentance has affected his actions. As far as I can see, Jesus' offer of friendship and acceptance is what has changed him, not the fear of punishment.

When we invite someone to follow Jesus, we need to remember that it's just that: an invitation. True, there are consequences to saying 'no', but Jesus will not force us to follow him, or to choose his path for our lives. He invites us into a restored love relationship; but love must be free; it cannot be forced, or it is not real love.

It's worth considering what it really means to choose his path – to become a disciple of the rabbi Jesus. We so often want to work out the steps of our own lives, forgetting that the One who created us knows what and who he has designed us to be. We need to be connected with him to live out our God-given purpose. But what if his purpose doesn't seem to be working out as we would like? Are we scared he might ask us to do something we don't want to do – go on the mission field, enter into the ministry, be single (or married!)? Can we wait in patience when prayers are seemingly unanswered, trusting him for his perfect timing and choices – his love – for us? His perfect plan for our lives may not be shaping up to our ideas of perfection!

If you imagine your life as a car, who is driving? Are you going your own way, even though you know it may not be in the direction Jesus wants for you? I believe if we block out his instructions, it can be rather like seeing Jesus sitting in the passenger seat; if we choose to go our own way, he will be with us because he has promised never to leave us – but he won't actually be 'driving'. Allow yourself a couple of moments to think about the possible consequences. Why not hand the steering wheel over to him?

When we view our lives from the perspective of eternity, what will we see? Generosity, love … or selfishness? We all make mistakes, but if we can, we should try to 'make good' any wrongs and live in peace with one another.

PAUSE FOR THOUGHT
Imagine you are walking up a staircase, but it peters out, ending in a wall. Then you see a parallel staircase, carrying on to unimaginable heights. Which staircase do you feel you are on? Which do you want to be on?

WATCH: 1:11-1:15:13

The church bells are ringing, and the charwoman, Mrs Dilber, finds a changed Scrooge. He's laughing, he's happy just to be alive. It's Christmas Day and he hasn't missed it. Everything is as it was; except that he himself is different. Happiness has drowned out humbug!

One of the things I like best about this amusing clip is when he dances around saying he doesn't 'know anything' and never has done! In my experience, this is certainly true when we walk with Jesus. The more I go on with him, the more I realise that there are many mysteries to which only God has the answer!

The clip ends with Scrooge giving a frightened Mrs Dilber a guinea for a Christmas present. She obviously expects very little out of life and thinks initially that the money is for her silence! Then Scrooge raises her wages. Ebenezer is already beginning to make a difference in people's lives by showing generosity and kindness.

THINK ABOUT

Sometimes the circumstances of life may make us feel as if we want a change – where we live, a job, a ministry. Or maybe we are reviewing a relationship, and we'd like someone else to change! I think it's easy to look at other people and wish they were different – 'if only she wouldn't …' 'if only he would …' It's so much harder to look in the mirror and see what we could change about ourselves. However, our own different attitude could have a potentially profound effect on others. Just as our negativity can impact them, so can a complete change of heart!

As we know, in this movie, Scrooge has a series of supernatural experiences and finishes up a changed man because of them. However, it's hard to 'change' and keep it up. We can make a decision to live differently, unselfishly, and start off well, but discover our fine resolve disappearing like the morning mist. For example, how many of us make New Year resolutions but find it difficult to keep up the good intentions? That gym subscription, that healthy diet; we might be keen in January, but what about in July? We may decide we need to not lose our temper so much in the New Year; be kinder; be more optimistic – but how do we actually implement that?

In truth, we may be able to adjust some of our behaviours, and deeds of great altruism can be born out of compassion. But what about our essential nature – the way we actually are as people? Must we admit that we need help?

A true heart change comes from connection with God. He is the only one who can really change our innermost nature. Ezekiel 36:26 tells us that he can take away a 'heart of stone' and replace it with a 'heart of flesh'. Jesus spoke about being 'born again' in his conversation with the Pharisee Nicodemus, who came to him secretly at night. In John 3:5-6 Jesus explains how we cannot enter God's kingdom unless we are born of the Spirit. It's the Spirit himself living in us, giving us a fresh, new life, who enables us to live to please God; to live the life of love that Jesus requires. We simply cannot do this in our own strength. As we read in 2 Corinthians 5:17: 'Therefore, if anyone is in Christ, the new creation has come: the old has gone, the new is here!' In short, our old sin nature has been nailed to the cross – that we may enter newness of life.

PAUSE FOR THOUGHT
Have you asked Jesus to change your heart?

WATCH: 1:15:14-1:17

Scrooge's next act of kindness is to look out of the window as he hears the bells, calling down to a passing boy, and instructing him to buy the prize turkey from the butcher's. He is very complimentary about the boy – his view of people has completely shifted! He offers him a shilling to buy the turkey and come back with the butcher, more if he can do it quickly. Scrooge's intention? To send this turkey anonymously to the Cratchit family.

When they receive it, sweet-natured Tim is the one who believes it might have come from Scrooge. What might have effected this change? Christmas …?

THINK ABOUT

Do you think and speak well of people? Or do you grumble about them, to yourself and others? Gossip is such a powerful weapon of the enemy. For a start, it can split up friendships (Proverbs 16:28; see also Proverbs 11:13; 20:19; 26:20). We can dress it up any way we like, but gossip can be really damaging.

It's so easy to criticise others, even under the pretence of wishing them well: 'We need to pray for so-and-so, do you know what she's done? She's …' In the clip we have just watched, Scrooge speaks well of a young boy – true, only to himself; but we can see here that he has a new attitude towards people.

Hearing criticism made about us when we are not present is, I think, far worse than a direct remark – even if it is hurtful – especially if the source is someone we consider a friend, and they have spoken negatively about us to someone else. It undermines trust and is also deeply disappointing. If we have a problem with somebody, let's be careful when we share it with a third party. It can be tricky to bring an issue up with someone face-to-face, but far better than gossiping or criticising behind their back.

If possible, we need to be careful to speak well of people. The old saying 'misery loves company' (apparently originating from Sophocles) is very apt. Let's be cautious if we forge 'friendships' with people who seem to delight in gossip. If they are talking about someone else, they are very likely going to talk about us to somebody! Ephesians 4:29-32 exhorts us not to give in to 'unwholesome talk' but to make sure that what we say will build up other people. We need therefore to make sure we don't deal in slander and malice but are compassionate and kind to others; often referred to as the 'Golden Rule', we should aim to treat people as we would like to be treated ourselves (Matthew 7:12). So let's be forgiving in our words as well as our actions – after all, God forgave us in Jesus.

PAUSE FOR THOUGHT
Do your words build up, or tear down?

WATCH: 1:17:04-1:19:42

Next, the penitent Scrooge turns up at his nephew's house. It isn't too late to accept the dinner invitation. He asks Fred's wife for forgiveness, which she willingly grants. Then he joins in the celebrations, dancing the polka. He's a very different man to the one we met at the start of the film!

THINK ABOUT

This short clip is entertaining, although it's also very touching. Watching Ebenezer Scrooge dance is such fun. I couldn't have imagined the grim character we saw eating his gruel alone earlier on in the movie, dancing with a girl and enjoying himself!

It hasn't been too late to accept the invitation

– forgiveness has been asked for, and received. Actually, I can't imagine Fred would have turned Scrooge away, even without the gracious humility his uncle displays when he meets Fred's wife, can you?

Jesus' invitation to 'come' is for everyone. He won't turn anyone away who comes to him (John 6:37). In the book of Revelation, we read the wonderful invitation to 'come' – anyone who is thirsty may 'take the free gift of the water of life' (Revelation 22:17; see John 4:14).

While we have breath, while we live, it is never too late! Jesus can give us abundant life in the innermost part of being; that's true happiness, one that isn't based on life's shifting circumstances (John 10:10). True contentment is found not in the insecurity of 'things', but in right relationship with God. Jesus in Matthew 6:19-21 talks about the transience of this life; he encourages us to store up 'treasures in heaven', not on this earth, where things can be enjoyed fleetingly, but then are gone. The thought of 'moths' and 'vermin' destroying earthly treasures makes me think of hoarding things up until they can be of no use to anyone. How much better to release blessing for the benefit of others.

Verse 21 tells us that our hearts will be where our treasure is located. Where's your heart today?

PAUSE FOR THOUGHT

Scrooge knocks on Fred's door and receives forgiveness and welcome. In Revelation 3:20 we read of Jesus knocking on the door of the heart. Although we often use this verse when speaking to people about following Jesus, in context, Jesus is knocking on the door of the *believer's* heart. Is he knocking on your door? Can you imagine what would happen if you opened it? What might he say? How might you reply?

WATCH: 11:20-1:23:15

In the last scenes, we see Scrooge playing a joke on his clerk – pretending to be annoyed by his lateness, but then increasing his salary. He wants to help Bob raise his family, if possible. Bob Cratchit's rather stunned expression indicates he certainly didn't expect that!

Scrooge admits he doesn't deserve his new-found happiness. But can he help it? No! He has a second chance at life.

As the film draws to a close, we learn that Ebenezer's heart-change affects others enormously. Tim doesn't die, he gets well; Scrooge becomes like another father, a far cry from the man at the start of the movie, who wants to be 'left alone'. He has brought happiness to others and enjoys a fulfilling new life as a result of his drastic change. The movie finishes to the strains of the beautiful carol, *Silent Night* ... which happily lacks the rather menacing overtones of *Hark! the Herald Angels Sing*, at the beginning!

THINK ABOUT

Scrooge doesn't deserve a second chance. None of us do. How wonderful of Jesus that he is willing to give it.

I'm not saying, though, that as we follow Jesus, our lives will turn out as happily as Ebenezer Scrooge's apparently did, after his spooky encounters. Following Jesus can be tough. Take a look at the book of Acts – miracles, but persecution. And, of course, we know that people are horrendously persecuted today for their faith in Jesus in many places in the world.

It can be difficult, too, when we have had a fairly dramatic life change to convince others that we are different – we are following Jesus now. We have been forgiven. Is it really that easy to wipe the slate clean? And what if someone has really offended us in the past, and comes to us glowing with new life, announcing they are now a Christ-follower? Can we be gracious in our forgiveness? What will that mean, potentially? Can (or should) a broken friendship, a relationship, always be restored?

Depending on the circumstances, although we can forgive, trust once betrayed can be very hard to regain. Also, it isn't always wise to take people at face value. We might have been praying for someone for a long time, and they eventually come to Christ and have a real turnaround. That can be a cause for great thankfulness, rejoicing and excitement. But what do we do if someone with whom we haven't always felt safe declares they are a 'new person'? Well, we need to be prudent, and exercise discernment. While believing the good, we have to be sensible and make sure we don't put ourselves in a potentially difficult or even dangerous position. Time will tell. The fruit of what someone really is, inside, will show. A changed life will manifest in many practical ways – as we see with Scrooge.

It's interesting to read the parable of the sower in Matthew 13. Some people who come to Jesus bear good fruit in keeping with their new life. Some don't: maybe the truth never takes root in the person; trouble for the sake of the gospel interrupts their life and they turn away; or life's worries and 'the deceitfulness of wealth' choke out what has been received with gladness. As Matthew 6:24 says, we simply cannot have two masters – we can't pursue God *and* material wealth (or any other 'idol'). Either will capture our hearts, so let's make sure it's Jesus: the One who came to earth to live and die for us, to bring us a life of depth and the riches of knowing him now and for eternity. Nothing, surely, compares with this.

So, we've come to the end of the story of Scrooge's supernatural wake-up call! Having been faced with who and what he really is, his awakened compassion means his once-hoarded wealth can be used for good as generosity flows from his changed nature. Likewise, as we are filled with the Holy Spirit, we are not to be stagnant pools; the 'living water' Jesus spoke of in John 4 flows up and out of us. Let's learn from the story of Scrooge to release what we have; being constantly filled ourselves, to overflow in blessing to others.

PAUSE FOR THOUGHT

It's not always easy to live for Jesus, but Philippians 4:13 says we can do all things in the strength he gives us. Maybe you are finding the Christian life tough. Ask God to fill you with his Holy Spirit today. Is there anyone you can share your problems with/pray with?

ADVENT CONNECTION

Read: Matthew 2:1-12

... Magi from the east came to Jerusalem and asked, 'Where is the one who has been born king of the Jews? ...'

When King Herod heard this he was disturbed ... he asked [the chief priests and teachers of the law] where the Messiah was to be born. 'In Bethlehem in Judea,' they replied, 'for this is what the prophet has written:

"'But you, Bethlehem, in the land of Judah ... out of you will come a ruler who will shepherd my people Israel.'"

Then Herod called the Magi secretly and ... sent them to Bethlehem and said, 'Go and search carefully for the child. As soon as you find him, report to me, so that I too may go and worship him.'

... they went on their way, and the star they had seen when it rose went ahead of them until it stopped over the place where the child was ... And having been warned in a dream not to go back to Herod, they returned to their country by another route.

Our last Advent Connection is with the Magi, otherwise known as the Wise Men. Traditionally we think of three of them, but the only evidence to support that number is in the gifts they bring. The Magi appeared some time after Jesus was born, so they aren't strictly part of the Christmas story. Yet, they always appear in nativity plays – and why not? The vivid symbolism of their gifts enriches our understanding that Christ was a King (gold), deity (frankincense) and would die (myrrh).

Jesus calls those who seek him from afar – and sometimes, we can feel far away from him, even when we have followed him for years. The spiritual 'desert' is a place with which many of us are familiar. Although the Spirit led Jesus into the wilderness (Matthew 4:1-11), sometimes, as with the prophet Elijah, we can put ourselves into this situation as a reaction to life's stresses (1 Kings 19:1-18), or as a result of poor choices. But regardless of how we came to be there, the wilderness is a place we may encounter God, rest, hear his 'gentle whisper', and be released into new things. However far we feel from God, we are never *too* far to simply 'come'.

It is interesting that the Magi were pagans; not the religious people of the Jewish nation we might suppose would be chosen to be among the first to greet God's Son. Jesus wasn't found in a palace, either. We noted earlier that God doesn't always act in ways we expect!

There's something in this account of the Wise Men's coming to seek for the new King of the Jews that I think we often miss. What if the Magi hadn't obeyed the warning in the dream? Matthew 2:16 tells us that when Herod realised the Magi hadn't done as he had asked, he was very angry – leading to a devastating bloodbath as he tried to wipe out the Messiah as a child.

Let's for a moment imagine, though, what would have occurred if the Wise Men had acted differently, if they hadn't heeded the warning and had instead returned to tell Herod where Jesus was. Jesus would have died as an infant. He wouldn't have grown up to show us what God is like and would not have died on the cross, bearing our sin. He would never have been raised from the dead, proving that all his words were true. There would be no all-embracing New Covenant. We would still be under the Law, with all its regulations. But in Jesus, we can have new life! How amazing it is that we have access to the Holy One; we can know him! Ephesians 2 tells us of what Jesus has done for us in wonderful detail. This is all undeserved grace from a merciful God who loves us so much.

So, the action of the Magi played a significant part in history. Their change of course changed *our* course.

We might make small changes in our lives, or large ones. Like Scrooge, we might feel we need a complete makeover – and for that, we must talk to Jesus! It's true that our actions can impact what happens in the future, positively or negatively; maybe not to the extent of the Wise Men's small-yet-not-so-small decision, but nevertheless, we underestimate the effect we could have on people and society as we look outwards towards others, and take selfishness off the throne of our lives.

So this Christmas, let's take the focus off ourselves and surrender to the King of kings, giving him his rightful place in our daily lives, remembering that without his first Advent, there would be no hope of his second coming.

Christ's Second Advent will not be like his first. This time, 'every eye will see him, even those who pierced him' (Revelation 1:7; see Daniel 7:13-14). Jesus, who came more than 2,000 years ago in humility, will come again in majesty: 'For the Lord himself will come down from heaven, with a loud command, with the voice of the archangel and with the trumpet call of God, and the dead in Christ will rise first' (1 Thessalonians 4:16). This is our real hope for the future. Jesus is the coming King of all.

Earlier in this book I mentioned how God spoke to me through a 'picture' of a leaky boat.

Jesus was in that boat, so would I choose to step aboard, or stay on the shore? Well, Jesus is my future, just as he is yours. When our time comes to leave this earth – whether through death, or if he returns before we die – it is Jesus who will be there. We need to trust him.

So my choice is that I would rather be in what appears to be a flimsy boat with Jesus than to remain on what seems to be the safety of the shore. The only place of real security and safety in this life is in and with him. He doesn't ask me to steer the course; he doesn't even ask me to row. He just invites me to be with him on the journey. I want to do that. How about you?

PAUSE FOR THOUGHT
- Do you feel far away from God? He's waiting for you to 'come'. What's stopping you?
- Is there some decision you need to make that might have a great impact on someone else – in your family, your street, your church, your community?
- What's on the throne of your life – or who?

ACTIVITY SUGGESTIONS

- If you remember the start of this chapter, we read part of Matthew 6. In what ways can you intentionally put Jesus first, during this Christmas season? Write down three ideas, however small. Small things can sometimes have big consequences!

- Maybe you know someone who is feeling far from God (and perhaps from other people: family members) this Christmas. What can you do to help them feel loved, remembered, included?

REFLECTION

God has a destiny for us; we are his creation, and he has prepared good things for us to do (Ephesians 2:10). He has a plan for our lives, as Jeremiah 29:11-13 asserts. But he also talks in the Jeremiah passage about seeking him fully – with all of our hearts. If we do so, he says, we will find him. What a wonderful promise. We need to look for him, spend time with him. Earlier, I mentioned I love birdsong. One morning, I was listening to the dawn chorus, but the sound of traffic on the main road beyond my garden was vying with the beauty of the song. Sometimes the 'traffic' in our lives threatens to drown out the voice of our loving God. Will you seek

him with all your heart, even in the middle
of the Christmas busyness?

PRAYER

*Lord of Glory, I worship you. You are the Lord of
time. The future is known to you. Thank you that
you have a plan for my life. Lord, I praise you
that you came to save us 2,000 years ago, born in
humility, and that you are coming again in power
and majesty. Thank you that you want me to know
you today, and have made that possible. Amen.*

CONCLUSION

So, humbug turns to happiness! Not just Scrooge's personal happiness, but the happiness of all around him; rather than sharing his gloom and misery with others, he releases blessing!

This timely and relevant story, essentially a challenge to review the attitudes of our hearts, has much to say to us, as I hope you have discovered – indeed, it may have spoken to you in areas we haven't even addressed here.

Christmas isn't about one day. It is a way of life. That's good to remember in the busyness of this time of year. 'Want' of many kinds are shown up in sharp contrast with the lavishness of the season. Let's not rush through the festivities without pausing and spending time to thank God for what we have, and to think about how we may reach out to those who are in lack, in whatever way, that we may serve them – not just now, but all year round. As we have seen, the story paints a picture of what

Christmas should look like as it is lived out in someone's heart. The only true Christmas spirit is that which is found in the Christmas child. Christmas, the festival, should really be about Jesus, but then, so should all of life. Advent is about remembering his first coming – being grateful for his presence – as well as looking forward to the time when he will come again.

The story of Scrooge encourages us not to just 'remember Jesus', perhaps as a cute baby in a manger, but to actually live out the life he has called us to. But true heart change is not something we can conjure up ourselves, for all our efforts. Neither is the Christmas spirit about feel-good personal intentions that desert us sometime towards the back end of January.

The spirits draw back a curtain on Scrooge's life revealing hurts that have had an ongoing effect. I wonder what it would look like if the curtain was drawn back on your life, or mine. One thing is for sure: what we experience, have experienced, and how we respond to it will affect us and those around us.

How far will we let our past experiences define us now? If we live too much in the past, it may lead to being locked into regret, or bitterness. Or it might be somewhere we find ourselves escaping to when real life gets a bit too much. Alternatively, if we live constantly in the future, we can experience untold agonies of fear and lose the sense of present peace. The only truly safe place is in the 'now' where God dwells with us. If we aren't present with him, and are too caught up with yesterday or tomorrow, then we may not hear what he is saying to us today. While holding in place the tension of past and future, let's make every effort to keep focusing on Jesus. God wants relationship, and in Christ, he has made it possible.

As you lay down this book, try to spend some time with God, listening for that quiet voice. Listen for him while you are putting up decorations, wrapping last-minute gifts, doing the washing-up. You could be amazed by how he can speak to you in the smallest things of life. Maybe, as soon as the festivities are over, the relatives have gone home and you are sitting down with a cup of coffee/tea/glass of wine, you will have time to reflect on your current choices and how they are affecting you and others.

There is no mention of Jesus' atoning for our sins in this story of Scrooge's repentant change of heart – which is, at least at first, perhaps motivated by a certain amount of fear, although genuine compassion sneaks up on him! But the greater change in a person comes when, drawn by his loving-kindness, they are connected with God through Jesus Christ. His own good works then flow in and through them, as their nature is changed to the likeness of Christ. However, it isn't only about what we do. It is about who we are – loved by God. This essential change of nature, and our own view of ourselves, resulting in freedom to live our lives as God intended, can only happen through the Spirit of God, living in us – the 'living water' promised by Jesus (John 7:38; Acts 1:4-5,8).

So, whether your experience of Christmas is generally humbug or happiness, thank God this Christmas that our future is assured when we know him, when we respond to his call to 'come'.

Do you know that assurance? His presence and comfort?

In the last chapter, I suggested you imagine two staircases: one ending nowhere, but the other going on to unimaginable heights. Put your hand in his today, and walk with him into the future he has for you. Although the Bible is clear about the consequences of ultimately rejecting him, he won't terrify us with images of the past or with what's to come, as we turn to him. He will forgive and forget (Hebrews 8:12), in a way we humans struggle to do. But then, he is God. The living God, the God of the past and the future, and the God of the 'now', where we experience him. Let's put our trust fully in him. He is faithful. He'll change our humbug to happiness ... if we let him!

IDEAS FOR GROUPS

1. If you have decided to share the Scrooge experience with friends, neighbours or relatives, why not hold a film evening, complete with popcorn, pizza and festive nibbles? Watch the movie and chat about it, using some of the Pause for thought ideas. You may wish to look at particular clips and thoughts in more depth. If so, pause the movie at the relevant points. The themes you might decide to explore could be around: supernatural interruptions; how the past affects the future – what would we change if we could; living fully in the present and what this means; the future – do we fear it, and what is the antidote to anxiety?

2. Alternatively, ask the group to think about the following discussion points:
   • The chains of life ... who put them there, and what can we do about them?

- 'You simply can't move forward while you are looking back.' True/false?
- Think about the potential problems of living too much in the past, or the future. How does each impact living in the present moment?
- Is it really possible for someone's essential nature to be changed? How? And by whom?

Then arrange to meet one evening (or afternoon) the following week, and ask the group what their thoughts have been around the film. Which of the discussion points interested them most, and why? Has God been speaking to them about anything they have watched? Some of the themes are very deep (for example, being bound by chains/rejection/forgiveness) so offer to spend time in prayer with anyone who requires it. If they need further help, try to facilitate that. This movie is about the possibility of change. Remind them that 'with God all things are possible', as Jesus asserts in Matthew 19:26. Hopefully, as people are open and honest, friendships will be developed further and there will be an increasing intimacy with God.

3. A third idea would be to look at the Advent themes in the book. If this is what you would like to do, watch the film and look at the 'Advent Connection' sections. Following on, you might like to arrange further meetings where your group can reflect on: Supernatural interruptions (Mary); the promised Messiah; Ordinary lives/extraordinary God (the shepherds); Choices (the Magi).

4. For each of the above, you can use the 'Prepare Yourself' ideas as icebreakers, or base starter discussions around them